# Sonic Boom, Light Speed and other Aerodynamics What Do they Mean? Science for Kids

## Children's Aeronautics & Space Book

# Do you want to be a pilot?

Here are some terms for basic aeronautics you should know.

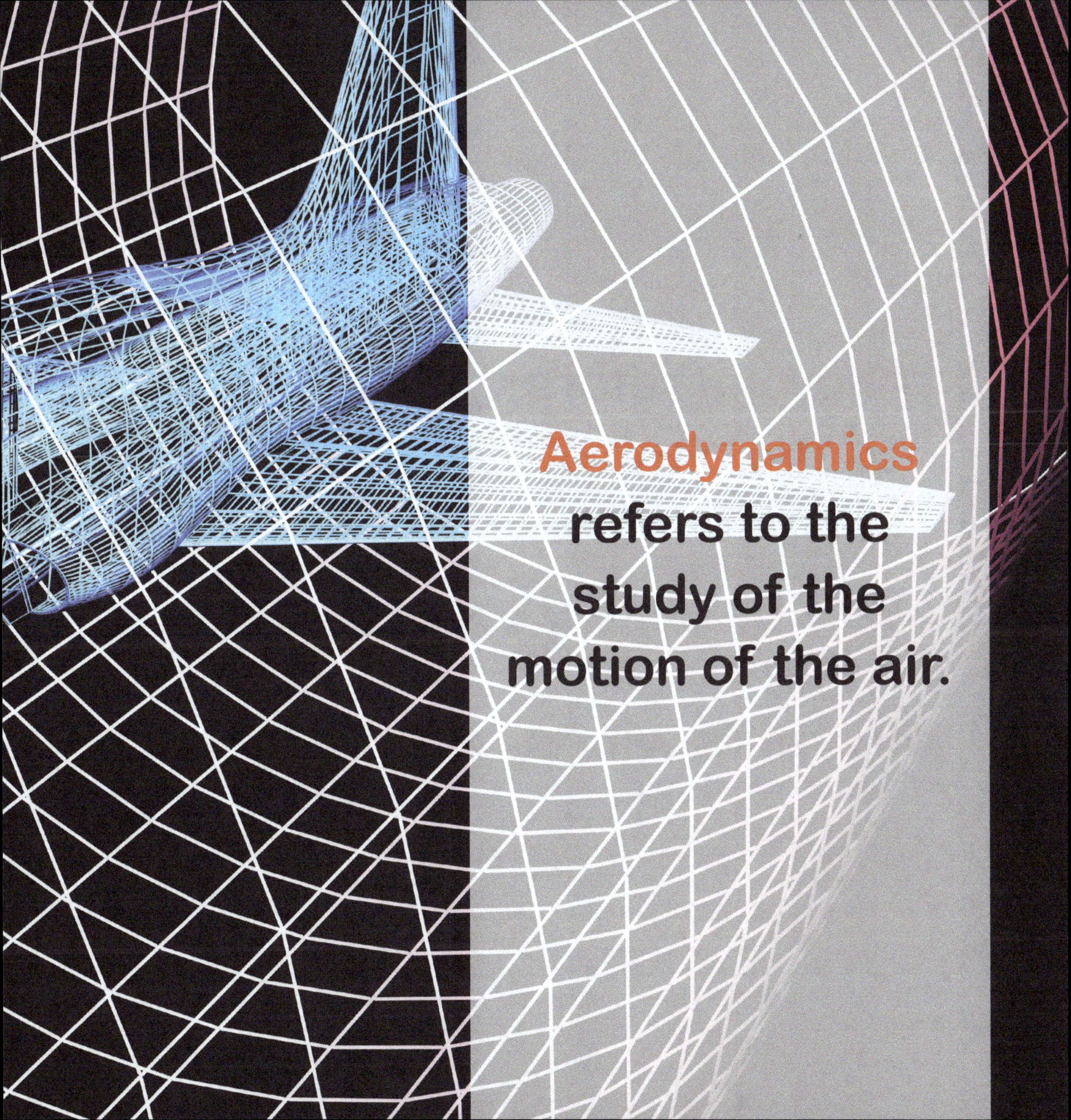
Aerodynamics
refers to the
study of the
motion of the air.

Ailerons refers to the control surface found on the trailing edge of an aircraft's wings.

**Aircraft** is a vehicle that travels through air.

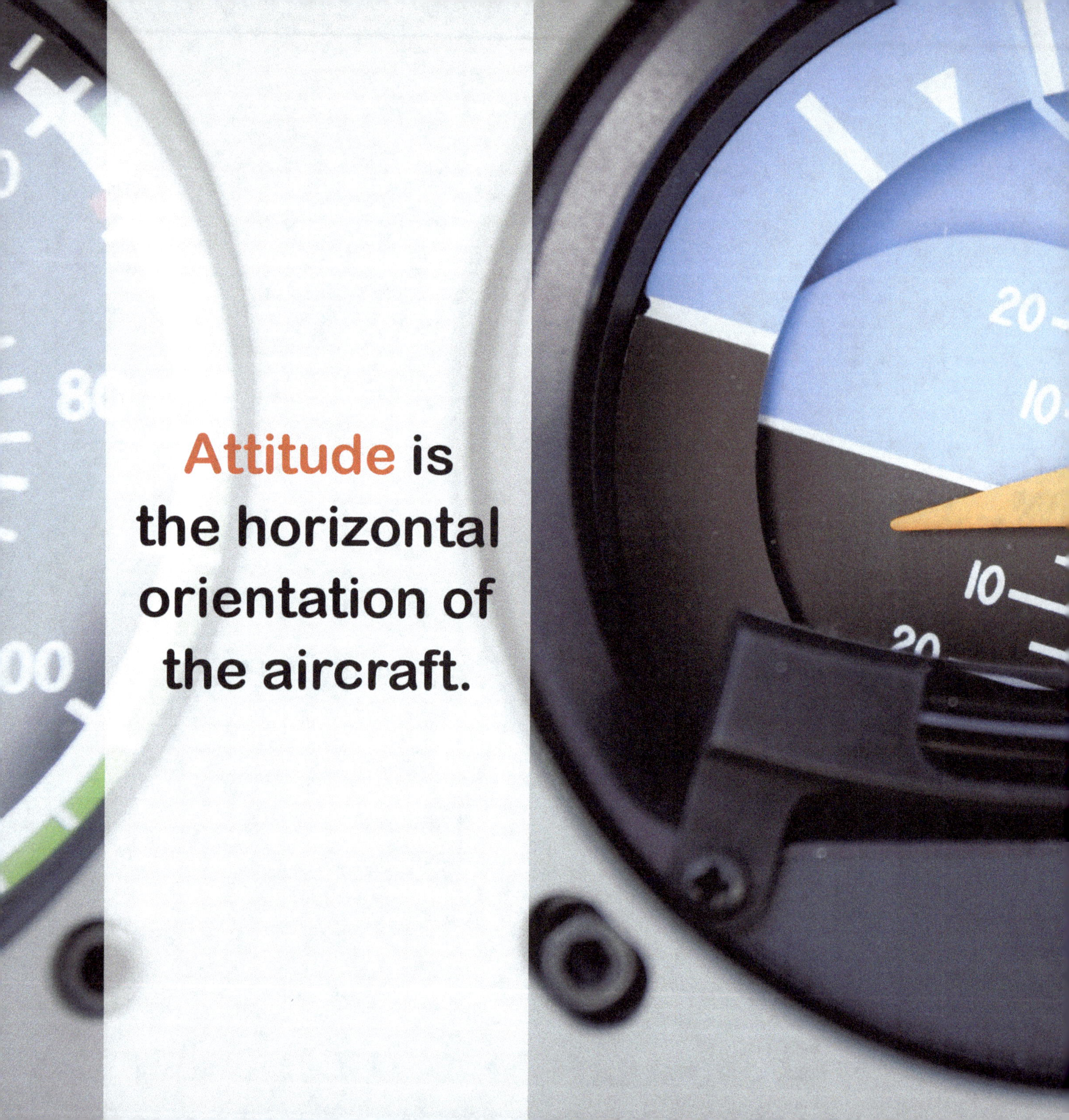

**Attitude** is the horizontal orientation of the aircraft.

20
10
8
1030
mb
1025
7

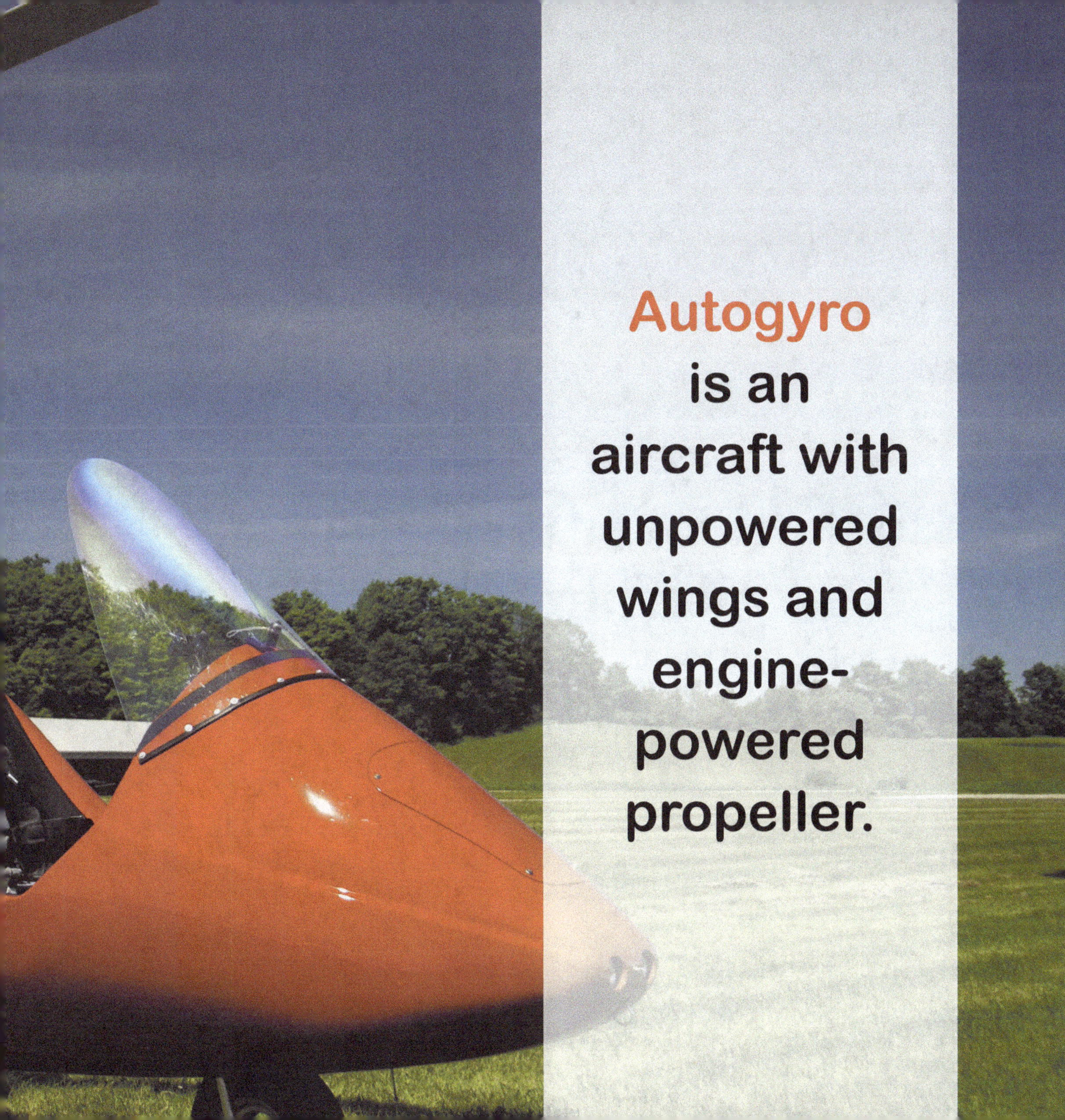

**Autogyro** is an aircraft with unpowered wings and engine-powered propeller.

**Aviator** refers to the pilot or a crew member of the aircraft.

Flight level
is the height
of an aircraft
above sea
level.

## Landing gear

**is the structure that supports the aircraft when not in the air.**

Light speed
refers to the
speed of light
while traveling
in vacuum.

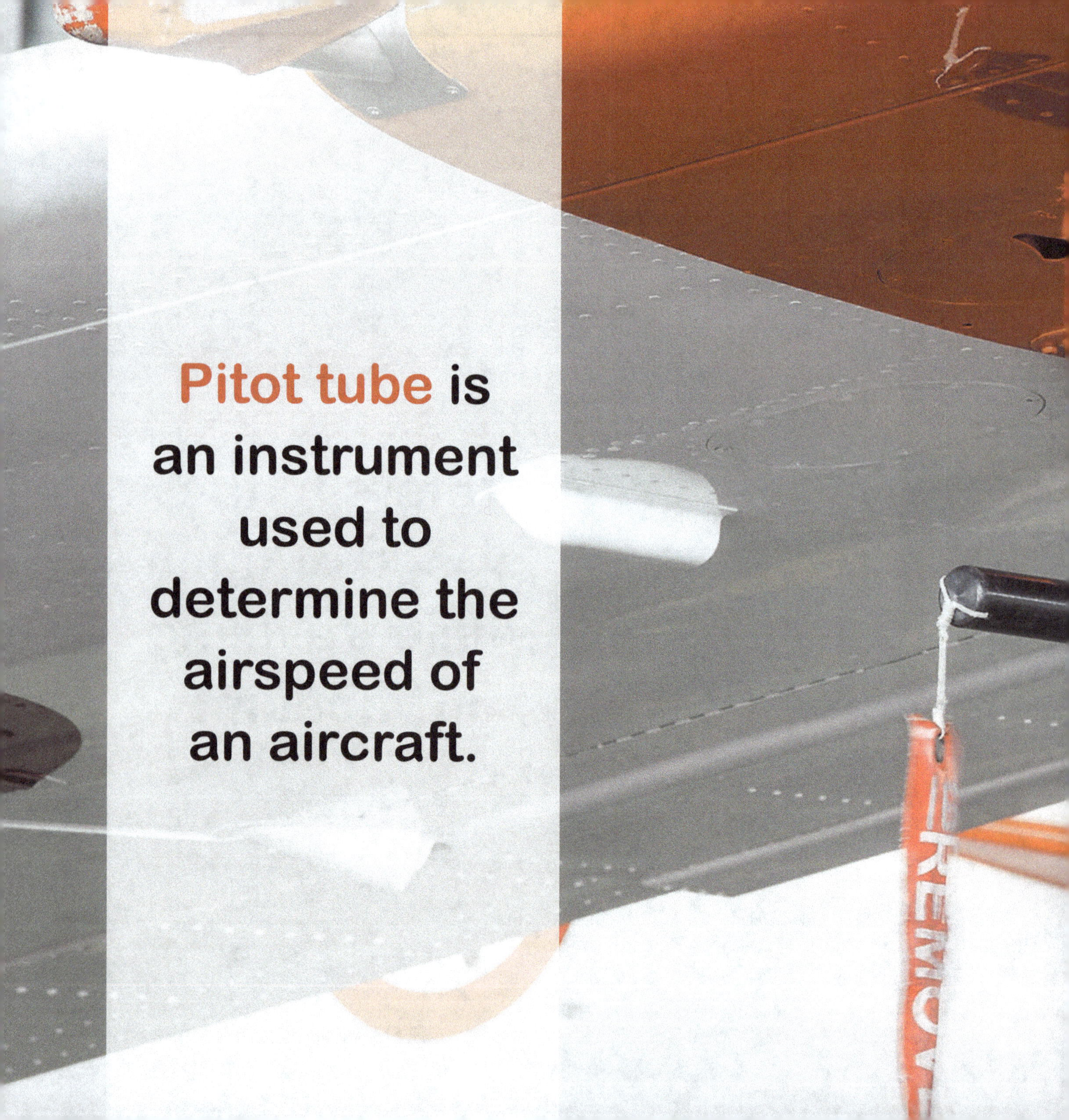

Pitot tube is an instrument used to determine the airspeed of an aircraft.

**Pressure altitude** is the denoted altitude on the altimeter.

**Sonic boom**
is the sound
created when an
aircraft passes
a series of
pressure waves.

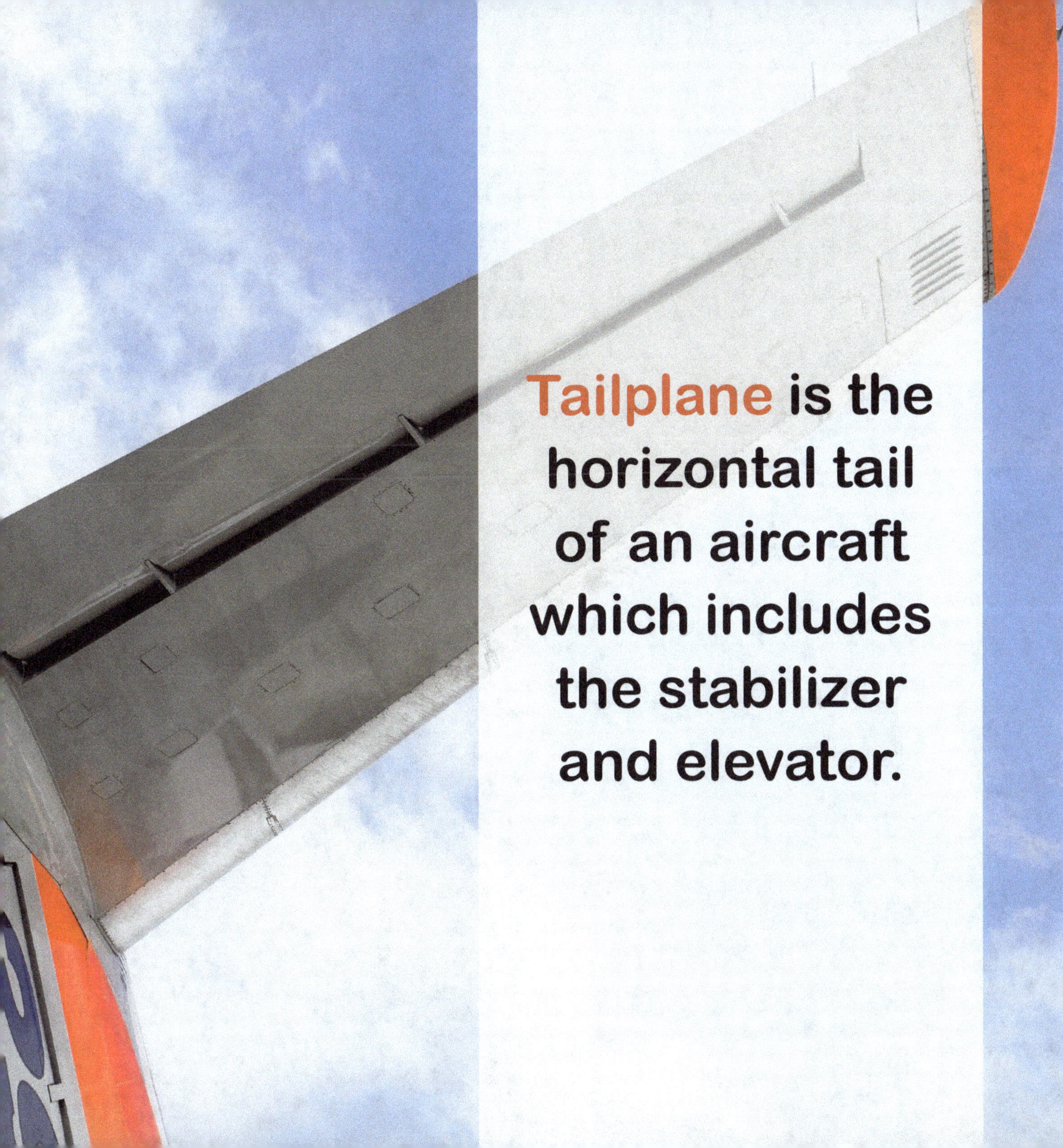

Tailplane is the horizontal tail of an aircraft which includes the stabilizer and elevator.

**Threshold** refers to the starting part of the runway used for landing.

Thrust is the force that causes the aircraft to move upward.

**Turbulence** refers to the sudden and violent movements of air.

Wind shear
refers to the
sudden change
of wind direction
or speed.

There are more aeronautic terms, research and learn. Have fun!

Visit
BABY PROFESSOR
EDUCATION KIDS
www.BabyProfessorBooks.com
to download Free Baby Professor eBooks
and view our catalog of new and exciting
Children's Books

www.ingramcontent.com/pod-product-compliance
Lightning Source LLC
LaVergne TN
LVHW060831170826
845678LV00010B/1957

* 9 7 9 8 8 6 9 4 4 5 1 0 0 *